The Mexican-American War

DON RAUF

Cavendish
Square
New York

Published in 2019 by Cavendish Square Publishing, LLC
243 5th Avenue, Suite 136, New York, NY 10016

Cataloging-in-Publication Data

Names: Rauf, Don.
Title: The Mexican-American War / Don Rauf.
Description: New York : Cavendish Square, 2019. | Series: Redrawing the map | Includes glossary and index.
Identifiers: ISBN 9781502635761 (pbk.) | ISBN 9781502635747
(library bound) | ISBN 9781502635754 (ebook)
Subjects: LCSH: Mexican War, 1846-1848--Juvenile literature.
Classification: LCC E404.R39 2019 | DDC 973.6'2--dc23

Editorial Director: David McNamara
Editor: Erin L. McCoy
Copy Editor: Michele Suchomel-Casey
Associate Art Director: Amy Greenan
Designer: Jessica Nevins
Production Coordinator: Karol Szymczuk
Photo Research: J8 Media

The photographs in this book are used by permission and through the courtesy of: Cover Science History
Images/Alamy Stock Photo, p. 4 Dikobraziy/Shutterstock.com; p. 9 David McNew/Getty Images; p. 11 MPI/
Getty Images; p. 13, 31, 43, 77, 86-87 North Wind Picture Archives; p. 15, 19 Bettmann/Getty Images; p. 20
Image courtesy of the Texas State Library and Archives Commission/Wikimedia Commons/File:Stephen F
Austin.jpg/Public Domain; p. 26 Ed Vebell/Getty Images; p. 34-35 Internet Archive/Wikimedia Commons/
File:NMW1946 D137 Capture of Santa Anna's private carriage.jpg/Public Domain; p. 37 FLHC/Alamy Stock
Photo; p. 38 David E. Scherman/The LIFE Picture Collection/Getty Images; p. 39 Peter Hermes Furian/
Shutterstock.com; p. 41 Kean Collection/Archive Photos/Getty Images; p. 49 American Stock/Getty Images;
p. 52 DeAgostini/Getty Images; p. 58 Mashuk/Digital Vision/Getty Images; p. 60 Library of Congress; p.
64 Niday Picture Library/Alamy Stock Photo; p. 66 SSPL/Getty Images; p. 69 LordRunar/iStockphoto.com;
p. 72 Paul Fearn/Alamy Stock Photo; p. 76 Everett Collection/Alamy Stock Photo; p. 80 DeAgostini/Getty
Images; p. 83 Nathaniel Currier/Wikimedia Commons/File:General Winfield Scott.JPEG/Public Domain; p.
89 Oxford Science Archive/Print Collector/Getty Images; p. 91 Library of Congress/Wikimedia Commins/
File:Treaty of Guadalupe Hidalgo, last page.jpg/Public Domain; p. 96 Bob Daemmrich/Alamy Stock Photo.

Printed in the United States of America

CONTENTS

Chapter 1   **Vast Expansion and a Show of Strength**   **5**

Chapter 2   **Manifest Destiny and Precursors to War**   **10**

Chapter 3   **Natural Resources in Disputed Territory**   **36**

Chapter 4   **The United States' First War on Foreign Soil**   **53**

Chapter 5   **The Final Fight, and New Borders Drawn**   **81**

Chronology   **99**

Glossary   **102**

Further Information   **104**

Bibliography   **106**

Index   **109**

About the Author   **112**

CHAPTER ONE

Vast Expansion and a Show of Strength

From 1846 to 1848, the United States fought a war with Mexico over disputed territory in the southwestern and western regions of North America. Before the war, lands that are now New Mexico, Arizona, Utah, Nevada, and California, as well as parts of Colorado, Wyoming, and Kansas, were all part of Mexico.

The war came at a time when many Americans were pushing for expansion: settlers were moving farther and farther west, and many wanted the United States to extend from "sea to shining sea." Some thought that it was America's destiny to acquire more land, a concept called Manifest Destiny. For believers in this notion, the United States was a country favored by God, one that could bring a better life and equality to all. American poet and essayist Ralph Waldo Emerson praised the country's virtues, calling it "the home of man." Destiny

Opposite: After the Mexican-American War, the United States established its southern border with Mexico and became a nation that stretched from sea to sea.

or not, the country saw that acquiring territory would add to its strength—and the Mexican-American War would bring about just that and reshape the southern border of the United States to resemble what it is today.

A Pivotal Moment in US History

The war was short, as Mexico found itself outmatched; the United States won almost every major battle. The two-year conflict was the United States' first war fought on foreign soil, during which its military achieved some important milestones. The war saw America's first amphibious landing—that is, a landing from the sea—and the country learned that massive firepower could achieve results that might spare soldiers' lives. The generals involved learned what it takes to launch a successful military campaign—skills many would go on to apply during the Civil War.

US commanders in the battlefield made their reputations and gained valuable military experience. Some of the war's most famous leaders included Robert E. Lee, Jefferson Davis, William Tecumseh Sherman, Stonewall Jackson, George McClellan, and George Meade—all of whom would go on to play critical roles in the American Civil War. Three military figures would go on to become US presidents—Ulysses S. Grant, Zachary Taylor, and Franklin Pierce. James Buchanan served as secretary of state during the war before becoming president. At the end of the Civil

War, when Lee met Grant during the South's surrender at Appomattox, Virginia, they recalled their first encounter during the Mexican-American War.

Key figures in US history also made their mark through their opposition to the war. Future president Abraham Lincoln built a reputation speaking out against it. Opponents to the armed conflict saw it as an unwarranted and overly hostile act toward another nation. Many said that President James K. Polk was needlessly antagonistic and provoked the war to gain territory.

If gaining territory was a primary motivation, then the United States achieved its goals. The end of the conflict with Mexico signaled the beginning of a new era that shaped the continental United States as we know it today. The United States increased its territorial holdings by one-third, and Mexico shrank to less than half of its former size. For the most part, the border between America and Mexico today is the same as the one agreed upon at the end of the Mexican-American War.

Continuing Tensions

The war increased tensions between Northern states, where slavery was illegal, and Southern slaveholding states, as controversy arose regarding whether newly acquired US territories might become slave states. The argument was that, as current slave states sought more land to expand their agricultural production, they might establish more slave states and tip the balance against the growing outcry against slavery.

Meanwhile, on the other side of the new border, many Mexicans felt they had been robbed of their land, and that fueled conflict between the two countries after the war had ended. In 1850, a group of Mexican writers gathered to share their perspectives on the significance of the Mexican-American War, called the *Guerra de 1847* or the *Guerra de Estados Unidos a México* in Spanish. Their words reflected the anger and betrayal many Mexicans felt as a result of the bloodshed and hostility:

> While the United States seemed to be animated by a sincere desire not to break the peace, their acts of hostility manifested very evidently what were their true intentions. Their ships infested our coasts; their troops continued advancing upon our territory, situated at places which under no aspect could be disputed. Thus violence and insult were united: thus at the very time they usurped part of our territory, they offered to us the hand of treachery, to have soon the audacity to say that our obstinacy and arrogance were the real causes of the war ...

TRADE ACROSS THE BORDER

The Library of Congress reports that over $1 billion worth of goods moves between the countries of Mexico and the United States every day.

US Customs and Border Protection estimates that about one million people legally cross between Mexico and the United States each day, making it the busiest border in the world.

The two countries nonetheless agreed on a border and began the process of living side by side as neighbors. The border, which extends some 2,000 miles (3,218 kilometers) from the Pacific Ocean to the Gulf of Mexico, is the most crossed international boundary. It continues to be a source of controversy, as politicians argue over how to best protect the border and prevent undocumented immigrants from entering the United States.

CHAPTER TWO

Manifest Destiny and Precursors to War

Ever since the United States won its independence from Great Britain in 1783, the new country had been driven to strengthen itself and to expand. After President Thomas Jefferson completed the Louisiana Purchase, acquiring a huge swath of territory from France in 1803, American settlers drove farther and farther west. East to west, this new swath of land stretched from the Mississippi River to the Rocky Mountains; and south to north, from the Gulf of Mexico to the Canadian border.

After defeating the British again in the War of 1812, US citizens and leadership demonstrated a growing confidence in the vision of a growing nation. When James Monroe became the fifth president in 1817, the United States entered what has been called the Era of

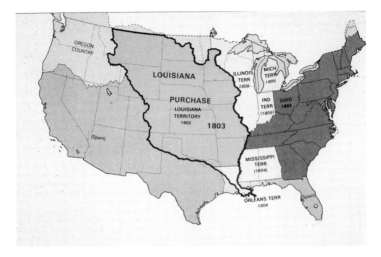

When President Thomas Jefferson purchased the Louisiana territory (*shown in green above*) from France in 1803, the United States nearly doubled in size. Spain, however, still controlled Florida and territory in the southwest and west (*shown in orange*).

Good Feelings, a time of unity and hope that lasted throughout Monroe's presidency, into 1825.

Early Battles for Territory, Power, and Freedom

Securing and populating new territory, and preventing European countries from further colonizing North America, were considered key to fortifying the country. During the first year of Monroe's presidency, US territory comprised only twenty states. Spain still controlled Florida, but its power there was collapsing; American settlers in western Florida were calling for independence. Although the Spanish Empire had begun colonizing Florida as early as 1565, it had, by the early nineteenth century, exhausted many of its resources fighting against France and its emperor, Napoleon Bonaparte. Spain and its allies defeated Napoleon in 1813, but the country now lacked financing to maintain a military presence in Florida.

Florida proved a dangerous place for many settlers with ties to the United States. The Seminole American Indian tribe was continually attacking US settlers. What's more, Florida had become a haven for runaway slaves, a situation that US slaveholding states did not appreciate; the Spanish would offer slaves freedom in return for their conversion to Roman Catholicism. In an attempt to recover these slaves and protect settlers, the United States sent troops into Spanish Florida. Andrew Jackson, soon to be elected president, led an incursion into the peninsula in 1817–1818 that became known as the First Seminole War.

Secretary of State John Quincy Adams saw an opportunity in the unrest in the region and Spain's dwindling control. He pushed for negotiations with the Spanish envoy to the United States, Luis de Onís y González-Vara. When the two countries came to terms in 1819 with the Adams-Onís Treaty, the United States took control of Florida. The price: the United States would cover about $5 million in claims by American citizens against Spain. Later, in 1845, Florida would officially join the Union as a slave state.

The Adams-Onís Treaty is sometimes called the Transcontinental Treaty because it also defined the

Although the United States gained control of Florida over Spain in 1819, it still waged a fierce war against Florida's Seminole Native American tribe, members of which are pictured here navigating a dugout canoe made of cypress in an 1800s woodcut.

boundaries between Spain and the United States in the west—an area that the two countries had disputed after the Louisiana Purchase of 1803. The agreed-upon boundary with what was then called New Spain ran along the Red, Sabine, and Arkansas Rivers up to the 42nd Parallel and then straight west to the Pacific Ocean. The Sabine River formed the eastern boundary for Spanish Texas. In addition, Spain gave up any claims to the northwestern region of North America.

After Adams-Onís was signed, Spain's viceroyalty of New Spain included what is today California, New

Mexico, Colorado, and Arizona. The United States also recognized Spanish sovereignty over Texas. Anastasio Bustamante, who would later become president of an independent Mexico, negotiated the southern border of Texas to be set at the Nueces River.

Slavery and Statehood

Under the Adams-Onís agreement, all regions of New Spain would still recognize the freedom of any American slave that crossed into its lands. Across the border, however, the fate of black or non-white individuals depended very much on the state in which they found themselves. Throughout the early 1800s, the issue of slavery threatened to divide the United States. The march toward abolition progressed steadily in the North, and by 1840, slavery had almost entirely disappeared in those states. In the South, however, slavery continued to be a primary economic driver and source of free labor.

With the slavery issue dividing the country, the status of each new territory that became a state weighed heavily on the federal government. In 1818, Missouri was poised for statehood, but the North wanted it to join as a free state while the South wanted it to become a slave state. Congress and the president agreed on the Missouri Compromise in 1820. The deal allowed Missouri to become a slave state, but slavery was abolished above the 36°30′ parallel in all regions of the Louisiana Territory.

An African American family held in slavery near Savannah, Georgia, is pictured in the 1860s. As the United States expanded, antislavery Northern states feared that newly added territories would join the Union as slave states.

Mexico's Fight for Independence

For Spain, however, troubles in the Western Hemisphere went beyond land negotiations with the United States. Just as US colonists had fought for their independence from Britain in 1776, Mexicans were now calling for a revolution against Spain.

A young military leader, Agustín de Iturbide, played an instrumental role in Mexican independence. Originally, Iturbide served Spain in Mexico as a royalist, dedicating himself to the Spanish cause and opposing revolutionary forces. However, Iturbide and other conservatives eventually changed course and made a grab for power. On February 24, 1821, Iturbide published the Plan de Iguala, calling for three major guarantees: that Mexico would be independent of Spain; that Roman Catholicism would be the religion of the land; and that Mexicans of Spanish descent (*mestizos*) would be united and equal to people born in Spain. Those with American Indian blood would have fewer rights.

Spain again found itself in a bind, lacking the manpower and resources to put down such a coup. On August 24, 1821, the last Spanish viceroy, Don Juan O'Donojú, signed the Treaty of Córdoba, accepting the Plan de Iguala and Mexico's independence.

The unity and equality called for in this declaration of independence, however, would not yet be realized. Iturbide, who saw himself as a great liberator, soon declared himself emperor. He silenced opposing views and surrounded himself with corrupt officials.

People throughout Mexico rose up against their new authoritarian ruler. Antonio López de Santa Anna led the rebellion, declaring the area around the city of Veracruz independent in 1822. Iturbide attempted to crush Santa Anna's insurgency, but leaders from other provinces joined forces with Santa Anna. Iturbide was forced to give up his crown less than a year after declaring himself ruler of an independent Mexico.

That same year, the Mexican congress established a constitution (partially modeled on the US Constitution) and began inching toward democracy. The constitution guaranteed basic human rights and separated the responsibilities of government between a central government and smaller states (*estados*). On October 4, 1824, the United Mexican States, or Estados Unidos Mexicanos, became a representative federal republic. The new republic, however, was bankrupt and ill-prepared for self-governance.

Mexico's Push for New Settlements

The land division agreed upon in the Transcontinental Treaty of 1819 now applied to the United States and the newly independent Mexico. Like the United States, Mexico wanted to strengthen itself as a country, and its leaders thought that encouraging settlement would help.

THE MONROE DOCTRINE

In 1823, US president James Monroe made it clear in the Monroe Doctrine that European colonization anywhere in the Western Hemisphere would not be tolerated.

Mexico invited immigrants from the United States and Europe to set up farms and raise cattle and granted them generous amounts of land in its northern provinces. In return, settlers had to join the Catholic Church and become Mexican citizens. Businessmen and speculators of European descent scooped up acres of land in Texas.

In the 1820s, Mexico established what it called an empresario system. Empresarios were settlers who could help establish bigger communities in Texas. Each empresario agreed to bring a set number of families to Texas within six years. In return, the empresario would receive 23,000 acres (9,308 hectares) for every hundred families settled. The new communities could maintain their own language, customs, and culture.

Mexico saw the empresarios as a way to offer some protection from attacks by Native Americans, as well. Raids by Comanches and other tribes who were the region's first occupants terrorized the newly arrived *rancheros*, or ranch owners. Although Anglo-American settlements were seen as a buffer, Comanches were still launching attacks on Mexican settlers as far as

This mural of an 1823 gathering of colonists on the Colorado River in Texas depicts Stephen Austin (*standing, in a black coat*) and Baron de Bastrop (*seated*), the Mexican government's land commissioner, doling out territories to newly arrived settlers.

500 miles (805 km) south of the Rio Grande river into the mid-1800s.

By late 1825, Stephen Austin had brought three hundred families to his Austin Colony in Texas. That number grew to nine hundred by 1829. Austin followed the rules for settling in Mexico: he and the

Known as "the Father of Texas," Stephen Austin took advantage of Mexico's land settlement policy, leading hundreds of families to colonize the region called Mexican Texas.

families who accompanied him all became Mexican citizens and converted to Roman Catholicism. Texas communities like Austin's sent representatives to the first Mexican congress, and for a long time, their relations with the Mexican government were good.

Anglo-Americans were not only attracted to the free (or very cheap) land in Texas, some also liked that Mexico had no reciprocal arrangement with the United States concerning debt collection or the return of criminals. Farmers who had defaulted on loans in America and were looking for an alternative to debtor's prison could begin again in Mexican Texas. Others believed that, in due time, Texas would be annexed by the United States, in which case their property would become more valuable.

On September 15, 1829, Mexican president Vicente Guerrero Saldaña, the first man of African heritage to be elected president of a North American country, emancipated all slaves in Mexico, but many communities in Texas sought and received an exemption. Roseann Bacha-Garza, program manager of the Community Historical Archaeology Project with Schools, which was founded in 2009 at the University of Texas Rio Grande Valley, says that thousands of slaves who escaped in Texas made their way across the Rio Grande to the land of the free—Mexico.

Tensions Rise in Texas

After Mexico enticed thousands to move to Texas, the nation began to question the loyalty of these new immigrants. Anglo-Americans soon outnumbered Mexicans two to one in the area. By one estimate, Texas had some thirty-five thousand inhabitants by the 1830s, most of whom were from the United States. Some Texans showed little regard for the Mexican government and even set up their own independent local governments.

A first attempt at secession took place between December 21, 1826, and January 23, 1827. Benjamin Edwards, the brother of empresario Haden Edwards, declared his community independent from Mexican Texas and proclaimed the area the Republic of Freedonia. Mexican military forces, led by Stephen Austin, quickly crushed the uprising.

Now, increasingly distrustful of settlers, Mexico passed a law blocking any additional immigration from the United States on April 6, 1830. However, despite this legislation, immigrants continued to stream in.

Soon thereafter, Anglo-American leaders in Texas gathered for the Convention of 1832, with Stephen Austin as its president. Representatives petitioned the Mexican government for more independence. They called for a lift on immigration restrictions, permission to form their own armed militia, and the right to form their own state, separate from the Mexican state of Coahuila y Tejas. The regional leader of the Mexican government called the convention illegal and rejected the resolutions, but he agreed to submit their grievances to the Mexican congress through proper channels.

For a while, these measures quelled the unrest, but as concerns went unaddressed, colonial leaders assembled again for the Convention of 1833. They put together a Texas state constitution to be submitted to the Mexican congress. The aim was not to bring about a total break with Mexico, but to increase self-rule.

The Texas Revolution

When Stephen Austin went to Mexico City on January 3, 1834, with a list of suggested reforms and the draft of a constitution, he was arrested and thrown in jail on the grounds that he was attempting to incite revolution.

In May of 1834, popular military leader Santa Anna dissolved the congress and state legislatures, declared himself dictator, and revoked the constitution of 1824. Many Texas settlers had liked this constitution, under which they were exempt from paying taxes for ten years after settling. The communities didn't receive any government services or military protection, but the Texans generally protected themselves, and they liked the status quo.

Austin had been loyal to Mexico for years and had made many attempts to keep the peace, but after spending a year and a half in jail, his allegiances changed. Upon returning in August of 1835 to the colony he had founded, Austin felt now that a fight against Mexico for Texan independence was inevitable. He headed to Washington, DC, to seek funding and military support to help the impending rebellion.

Two months later, the first conflict erupted in Gonzales. The Mexican government had given the town a small cannon in order to protect itself against local Native Americans. As tensions with the settlers mounted, Mexico asked the town to return the cannon. When they refused to surrender the weapon, Mexico sent in one hundred dragoons, or mounted troops.

Texans hastily assembled at least 140 men to confront the Mexican soldiers. The Texas militiamen taunted the Mexican soldiers, daring them to try and take the cannon. On October 2, 1835, the first shots of the revolution were fired. Texans ambushed Mexican troops and forced them to retreat. The confrontation made clear that Texans were now ready to fight for their independence.

Rebellions erupted in Texas, as well as in the Yucatan, the New Mexico Territory, and California. At first, Texans fought for the 1824 constitution and to overturn the ban on immigration, but many felt that Santa Anna's government had crossed a line and there was no going back: the movement in Texas was increasingly pro-independence. In 1835, Texas lawmakers officially assembled a peacekeeping force called the Texas Rangers.

With the War of Texas Independence underway, Austin was named the commander of Texan military forces. A few weeks after the Battle of Gonzales, he led a 400-strong battalion toward San Antonio, where Mexican forces of up to 650 waited. Houston and his volunteer army were able to drive the Mexican soldiers from the city. In the end, the Texans lost 35 men and the Mexicans lost about 150. Military experts attribute some of the Texans' success to the accuracy of their rifles.

Santa Anna did not take the defeat lightly and was determined to mount a ferocious response. Leading more than 7,000 men, Santa Anna marched northward toward San Antonio, crossing the Rio Grande in the cold winter at the beginning of 1836.

In the meantime, Stephen Austin was suffering from health problems and stepped down as the military's leader. Sam Houston, a friend of President Andrew Jackson's, replaced him. Hundreds of men were now heading from the United States into Texas to help fight for the cause of independence. Even frontiersman and former Tennessee congressman Davy Crockett traveled to the Alamo to fight for Texas.

"Remember the Alamo!"

At the Alamo mission in San Antonio, Colonel William B. Travis and Colonel James Bowie commanded about 150 soldiers and twenty cannons. Bowie had helped in the initial successful siege of San Antonio. (He would also become famous for his long-bladed weapon, which became known as the Bowie knife.) When Bowie returned to defend the Alamo, he said he would "rather die in these ditches than give up this post to the enemy." It turned out to be a prophetic statement.

By the time thousands of Mexican soldiers led by Santa Anna arrived on February 23, 1836, the number of Texan soldiers defending the Alamo had risen to only about two hundred men. Santa Anna and his men almost immediately reclaimed the city of San Antonio, surrounding the Alamo while Texan troops inside the mission prepared for attack. Santa Anna pounded the Alamo constantly with artillery for twelve days and nights. His plan was to give the Texans no rest and wear

During the Texas Revolution, two hundred men, including frontiersman Davy Crockett (*shown wearing a raccoon-skin hat*), held off thousands of Mexican soldiers at the Alamo for thirteen days until they were massacred on March 6, 1836.

them out before launching a decisive siege. Of course, this plan wore his men out, as well.

Although the Texans were able to hold them off for thirteen days, on March 6, Santa Anna ordered his men to take the Alamo in a three-pronged attack. The Mexicans successfully seized the Alamo, but the price in human lives was high. A battalion of 800 was directed to scale a wall—and only 180 of them survived. Much of the fighting was hand-to-hand combat with punches, knees, knives, lances, pikes, and pistols. In ninety minutes, every Texan soldier was killed, including Bowie and Crockett—but they had put up an impressive fight, killing 1,544 of Santa Anna's men. More than 500 lay on the ground wounded.

Although Santa Anna was reportedly pleased with the results, one of his men commented that another such win would be their ruin. The Alamo wouldn't be the last place where Santa Anna's military would pay a high price in lives lost.

For Texans, the Alamo became a symbol of heroism for the cause of independence and courage against insurmountable odds. Texans who continued the fight for independence would use the rallying cry of "Remember the Alamo!"

While the siege of the Alamo was underway, Texan delegates had gathered at Washington-on-the-Brazos, and by March 3, delegates were signing a declaration of independence. Eleven days after the defeat at the Alamo and San Antonio, a constitution was written and signed. Houston was confirmed as commander of the army.

The Goliad Massacre

The next few weeks were marked by a string of defeats for the Texans. Mexicans triumphed over commander James W. Fannin and his men at the Battle of Coleto on March 19 and 20, 1836. Fannin and about 300 of his men surrendered under the condition that they would be treated fairly as prisoners of war and returned as soon as possible to the United States. The Mexican commander accepted these terms and held them prisoner with other captured Texans at Goliad. Santa Anna, however, would not agree to clemency. He called them "perfidious foreigners" and ordered that they all be slaughtered. Records show that 342 were shot to death on March 27.

The Goliad Massacre turned the tide against Santa Anna. Instead of being seen as a cunning military leader, he was now perceived as utterly evil and ruthless. The senseless execution strengthened the resolve of Texans and Americans to win. "Remember Goliad!" became another cry of vengeance when Texans fought on the battlefield.

The Birth of an Independent Texas

In mid-March of 1836, Houston ordered that his men at Gonzales retreat along with civilians. He needed time to regroup and strategize. He wanted to find the most opportune moment to strike back. On April 21, Houston organized about 900 men and launched a surprise attack on Santa Anna and about 1,300 of his soldiers near the San Jacinto River, not far from the coast. As the Mexican troops were resting, hundreds of Texans swept in, rallying each other with cries of "Remember the Alamo!" and "Remember Goliad!" By all accounts, the attack was a bloodbath. In eighteen short minutes, the Texans had killed 630 men and imprisoned 730. Only nine Texans died. Santa Anna fled disguised as a common soldier, but he was soon captured. With the leader of Mexico imprisoned, Texans ordered his armies to retreat.

In exchange for his freedom, Santa Anna signed a peace treaty with the Texans at Velasco, ending the fighting. Santa Anna agreed that Mexico and the United States would exchange prisoners, that Mexico would no longer attack Texas, and that his country would return confiscated properties. Santa Anna also agreed that the southern border of Texas would be drawn along the Nueces River, rather than the Rio Grande, as the Texans argued it should be. In return, Santa Anna and Mexican troops could return unharmed to Mexico.

In January of 1837, Santa Anna was escorted to Washington, DC. President Jackson told him that the United States would give aid to Mexico if it recognized Texas as an independent country. After Santa Anna promised to do all he could to fulfill all the terms of the peace treaty, he was returned to Mexico.

It seemed for a short time that peace might prevail. The problem was that Santa Anna no longer represented his country. The Mexican government had unseated him and stripped him of power; his promises were worthless. On May 20, 1836, under a newly elected Anastasio Bustamante, Mexico declared void all of Santa Anna's actions as a captive. It refused to

WHEN TEXAS BECAME A COUNTRY

When Texas declared itself an independent nation on April 21, 1836, its land mass encompassed all of the present-day state of Texas in addition to portions of New Mexico, Oklahoma, Kansas, Colorado, and Wyoming.

Its eastern border, which was established with Spain, remained the Sabine River. The river today forms a boundary between Texas and Louisiana. According to the Daughters of the Republic of Texas, the border of Texas nation headed northwest at the Red River; then at the 100th meridian (a longitude line), cut north to the Arkansas River and present-day Dodge City, Kansas; then west to the headwaters of the Arkansas River, near present-day Leadville, Colorado; and finally, north to the 42nd parallel, near present-day Rawlins, Wyoming. From Silverton, Colorado, the western and southern boundary then followed the course of the Rio Grande.

The United States recognized the Republic of Texas as its own nation and continued to do so until it became part of the United States in 1845. As its own country, the republic even had its own currency: the Texas dollar, informally called the Texas redback.

Sam Houston was elected the first president of the so-called Lone Star Republic; on the same 1836 ballot, Texans voted 3,277 to 19 to become a state, and part of the United States. However, Congress delayed the decision on statehood for almost a decade because Texas would have joined as a slave state, disrupting the balance of power between the North and the South.

Meanwhile, the new Republic of Texas still had a geographic dispute with Mexico. The established southern border had been the Nueces River, but Texas drew its southern border at the Rio Grande (called the Río Bravo del Norte in Mexico). This border dispute would be one of the main reasons Mexico and the United States would again head to war.

Texas became the smaller size it is today with the Compromise of 1850. In this deal, Texas gave up much of its western territory to the United States in exchange for $10 million to pay off previous debts. These western territories would go on to form new states.

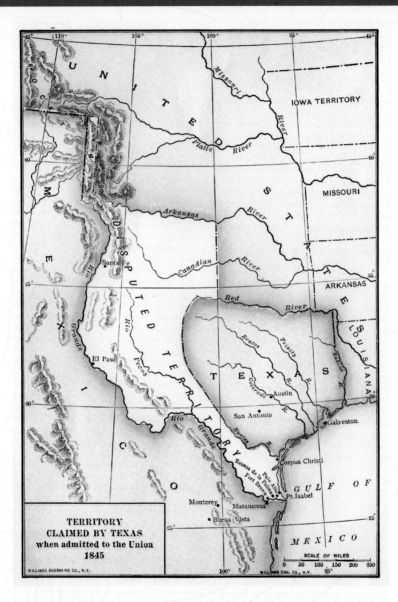

TERRITORY
CLAIMED BY TEXAS
when admitted to the Union
1845

WILLIAMS ENGRAVING CO., N.Y.

SCALE OF MILES
0   50   100   150   200   250

Mexico disputed the land claims of the Republic of Texas (*shown in orange above*). Disputed territory is shown in yellow, and Mexico is shown in pink in this 1845 map.

recognize an independent Texas, including a southern border at the Rio Grande.

Deep Debt and the Pastry War

Beyond dealing with Texas and trying to maintain control of its territories to the north, Mexico faced the mounting challenge of repaying its debt.

After winning its independence in 1821, Mexico entered a period of unrest on many fronts. It had twenty leaders in twenty years, as military leaders and others fought for power. In 1828, forces loyal to Mexican president Manuel Gómez Pedraza y Rodríguez and supporters of opponent Vicente Guerrero Saldaña fought in the streets of Mexico City. During the turmoil, some Mexican soldiers looted shops in the Parián marketplace. The thriving shopping center never recuperated. One of the businesses ransacked in the chaos was a pastry shop owned by a French citizen known only as Monsieur Remontel. He petitioned the Mexican government to pay him for damages, but the government found his demand for 60,000 pesos to be outrageous; his business was valued at only 1,000 pesos.

After years of trying to get compensation from Mexico, Remontel turned to France. The request, which made it all the way to King Louis-Philippe, triggered France to pursue collection on all unpaid debts owed by Mexico—a total of 600,000 pesos.

According to *The Encyclopedia of the Mexican-American War*, the Mexican government had borrowed millions from French banks and imposed a forced loan on foreign businesses to pay for the battle against Texas in 1836. France threatened that if Mexico did not pay up, it would take military action.

In April 1838, French warships formed a blockade in the port of Veracruz. The United States aided France, sending a schooner to help with the blockade. The blockade cut off a vital channel of trade and funds for Mexico. The uneasy standoff continued for months until France bombarded the fortress of San Juan de Ulúa with cannon fire on November 27, 1838. Mexico then declared war. France quickly overcame Mexican forces, capturing almost the entire navy.

Santa Anna, meanwhile, saw the war as a chance to reclaim his glory. He organized his own small group of soldiers to attack the French. During a skirmish that drove some French forces back to their ships, he was sprayed with buckshot, and his leg had to be amputated. His valor helped him regain the presidency in 1842, and once he was leader again, he staged an elaborate state burial for his amputated leg, parading his shriveled appendage from Veracruz to Mexico City. In 1847, during the Mexican-American War, Santa Anna would leave his prosthetic leg behind on the battlefield. For the Americans, the leg would become an iconic trophy. Today, it's on display at the Illinois State Military Museum in Springfield.

General Antonio López de Santa Anna's private carriage (and wooden leg) were captured during the Mexican-American War and kept as a symbol of the American victory.

The Pastry War lasted about four months, until finally, Mexico sought the help of Britain, which helped negotiate a peace deal in March 1839. The fighting ended, and Mexico agreed to pay the 600,000 pesos in compensation.

In addition to owing France, Mexico owed $3 million in payment and damages to the United States for harm and property resulting from its battle with Texas. Mexico's inability to pay back the debt would become one of the justifications for the Mexican-American War.

CHAPTER THREE
Natural Resources in Disputed Territory

After Texas achieved independence in 1836, both Texas and Mexico claimed the 200-mile (322-km) stretch south of the Nueces River and north of the Rio Grande to be theirs. For more than a decade, Texans and Mexicans populated the area and considered it their own. The matter of who would control the land permanently would be settled by the Mexican-American War, ten years later. The rivers, however, would not be the only key resources to drive the ongoing land dispute between the United States and Mexico; from gold and grazing lands to Pacific ports and whale oil, the land once belonging to New Spain and Mexico was a bountiful source of wealth—something the United States wanted to claim for itself.

In 1845, General Zachary Taylor assembled American troops at Corpus Christi along the Nueces River before marching south to the Rio Grande, a waterway that the United States desperately wanted to control.

Life-Giving Rivers

Called the Trans-Nueces, also known as the Nueces Strip and the Wild Horse Desert, the actual land between the two rivers was considered something of a wasteland. However, both countries saw value in controlling the Rio Grande, which was much larger than the Nueces River and led all the way from the

The Rio Grande and its tributaries bring life-sustaining water to create fertile crop-producing lands in an area that is otherwise very dry.

Rocky Mountains to the Gulf of Mexico. At a length of 1,185 miles (1,907 km), the Rio Grande is the second-longest river in North America after the combined Mississippi and Missouri Rivers, and the twentieth-longest river in the world. The Nueces, on the other hand, is only 315 miles (507 km) long.

WHAT'S IN A NAME?

Nueces is Spanish for "nuts." The river got its name from all the pecan trees growing along its banks.

Today, the Rio Grande river forms the border between Mexico and Texas, flowing toward the southeast for more than 1,200 miles (1,930 km) from El Paso to the Gulf of Mexico.

Starting in south-central Colorado, in the San Juan Mountains, the Rio Grande flows south into New Mexico, through Albuquerque. Today, after cutting through New Mexico for about 470 miles (756 km), the river becomes the border between Mexico and the United States in El Paso and continues for some 1,240 miles (1,996 km) until it reaches the Gulf of Mexico. The river separates Texas from the Mexican states of Chihuahua, Coahuila, Nuevo León, and Tamaulipas.

Along its journey from mountains to sea, several major tributaries feed it—the Pecos, Devils, Chama, and Puerco Rivers in the United States and the Concho, Salado, and San Juan Rivers in Mexico. Brownsville, Texas, and Matamoros, Mexico, straddle the river's mouth at the Gulf of Mexico.

Some small steamboats have traveled upstream to Rio Grande City, and at times as far as Roma, when the river was high. Overall, however, the Rio Grande is unnavigable except near its mouth, so it has not been important in terms of trade.

Bountiful Harvests

Both Mexico and Texas saw the value of the Rio Grande's river basin—about 8,000 square miles (20,720 sq km). This land, fed by the river and its tributaries, could become a rich agricultural region in an area that was otherwise very dry and prone to drought. The river had already proven to be a vital artery for crop cultivation; the Pueblo Indians, early inhabitants of the region, saw the value of the river for irrigation and farming purposes. As early as 1540, the Spanish explorer Francisco Vázquez de Coronado reported that Native Americans had developed an irrigation technique drawing upon the river waters to raise crops in this arid land. The Pueblos thrived along its northern banks in what is today Las Cruces, New Mexico. The Caddo Native American tribe figured out

The Pueblo Indians developed irrigation systems along the Rio Grande, which helped them raise abundant harvests of corn, beans, and squash.

how to cultivate corn, beans, and squash in the area, supplementing their crops with hunting and gathering. The Nueces River, too, brought life-sustaining water that was crucial in terms of agricultural development.

It's estimated that the Rio Grande brings water to some 2.1 million acres (849,840 ha) of cropland, with just over half on the Mexican side and the remainder in the United States. Dams along the river have been able to create important life-sustaining reservoirs.

The river has enabled people in the Colorado area to raise alfalfa and potatoes. New Mexican farmlands have produced grapes, pecans, and cotton. The delta-valley region of the lower Rio Grande has proven to be fertile ground for growing vegetables, citrus fruits, and cotton. And although it's not a major business, fishing has also provided sustenance for people around both the Rio Grande and the Nueces.

Today, the United States and Mexico share the water of the river under a series of agreements administered by the International Boundary and Water Commission. The commission manages water supplies, water quality, and flood control in the border region.

The Value of a No-Man's-Land

While not all land in the Trans-Nueces was suitable for agriculture, much of it was good for ranching. Although the Nueces Strip was mostly scrub- and cactus-covered, cattle could still feed in these lands. The word "ranch" comes from the Mexican-Spanish term *rancho*, which refers to a large grazing farm where horses and cattle are raised. Ranching in Texas is said to date back to the 1730s, when herds of cattle were allowed to roam freely near San Antonio and Goliad. Before the Mexican-American War, Mexico had opened large tracts of public land for raising cattle and other animals. It was not easy work. In southern Texas, as in many regions of the West, ranchers faced regular raids by Native Americans. In the late eighteenth and

The grasslands and prairies of Texas have been well-suited to raising cattle. Ranchers have thrived here for years, nurturing their livestock on vast, open stretches of land.

early nineteenth centuries, early ranchers built strong compounds as a protection against these attacks. Mexican rancheros established livestock production operations, opening establishments with names such as Ojo de Agua, Las Mesteñas, La Parra, and Santa Gertrudis.

Beyond agriculture, the lands around the Rio Grande have been valued for their mineral resources—petroleum, natural gas, coal, uranium, silver, lead, gold, potash, and gypsum. The Spanish had started mining communities as early as the late 1500s in the upper Rio Grande region, in what is today New Mexico. The real mining boom would not come until the late 1800s.

Meanwhile, another territory once belonging to Mexico proved to be a source of wealth as well. While Mexico was finalizing its peace treaty with the United States, a game-changing discovery was made in California. On January 24, 1848, James W. Marshall found gold at Sutter's Mill in Coloma, California, near Sacramento. News of the discovery spread fast, and the United States soon had gold rush fever. Hundreds of thousands of people packed up, left their lives behind, and headed to California, lured by the prospect of getting rich. In San Francisco, many workers in the shipyards, newspapers, and elsewhere quit their jobs and headed to the hills to search for gold. The huge group of hopeful miners who arrived in 1849 came to be called the '49ers. California was bustling with activity as thriving mining towns popped up. By 1850, however, the fever was cooling as the gold that was easy to find on the surface had, for the most part, already been claimed. The independent miner struggled as industrialized mining operations took over; many of those who had set out as hopeful adventurers became wage laborers in the mines.

Today, regions in the West and Southwest are leaders in mineral production. In a 2017 report from the United States Geological Survey, California, Texas, Arizona, and Nevada were the top four states in the United States in terms of producing valuable minerals. Mexicans, and Spaniards before them, had some idea of this wealth, but they did little to exploit the mineral resources on their northern frontier—the area would later be revealed to hold vast amounts of gold, copper, and silver. Today, Nevada leads the nation in gold mining, with silver mining close behind. Arizona is the top copper producer. California, meanwhile, has an abundance of boron, which is used in glass and ceramics.

The Untapped West

The territories of the West and Southwest offered vast resources with lands that were prime for cultivation and rich in mineral resources. New Spain and, later, independent Mexico included California and the southwestern portion of the United States. In the latter half of the eighteenth century, Spain built missions in these areas as a means of colonization. The

Spanish missions were frontier outposts that sought to incorporate native people into Spain's colonial empire and convert them to the Catholic religion. At first, they were a reaction to Russian trappers who, in the 1760s, were moving farther and farther south along the West Coast, to as far as where San Francisco is today. However, these outposts just scratched the surface when it came to tapping the region's immense wealth; while Spain and Mexico controlled these western lands, they were not taking much advantage of them.

Franciscans (a religious order within the Catholic Church) set up all the missions in New Spain. The Franciscans considered the Native Americans godless souls who needed to be saved. Spain knew that individuals and soldiers who attempted to control indigenous populations were often met with antagonism, but it believed that the Catholic Church would have more success. What's more, New Spain and Mexico found it hard to persuade settlers to go into some of these vast wilderness regions, and the Franciscans were willing to do just that. To protect the missions, the rancheros, and the mines, Spain established *presidios*, military forts where soldiers were stationed.

The hope was that missionaries could bring order to various regions in the New World through an organized daily life of prayer, work, meals, and relaxation; they would all work together to cultivate the land and raise livestock. This lifestyle was often imposed upon native peoples against their will; often, tribes were forcibly taken and placed into the mission system. After the Native Americans had accepted the Spanish lifestyle and religion—the Spanish believed—the community could transition to a secular arrangement operated under colonial law.

The missions had varying levels of success. About twenty-six missions were established within the borders of what would become Texas. A total of twenty-one were set up in California. Some achieved their goals—converting local people, cultivating the land, and raising cattle. The Coahuiltecans of southern Texas, for example, readily adapted to the system and welcomed Spanish protection and access to a plentiful food supply. In California, most of the missions were models of economic prosperity, and thirty thousand indigenous people were converted. Other missions failed. Warlike nomadic tribes such as the Apache and the Comanche refused to be converted. Meanwhile, the missions spread disease, and thousand of Native Americans died from exposure to unfamiliar illnesses that had been imported from Europe.

When Mexico gained independence, it feared that Spain would retain too much influence in its territories. In 1826, the Mexican governor of Californian freed natives from missionary rule and made them eligible to become full Mexican citizens. The goal was to make them self-sufficient and encourage them to settle down in pueblos that would be subject to the same laws and

THE CALIFORNIA COAST

While the coastal ports in California would prove to be very important in the war effort as strategic inlets for moving in troops, President Andrew Jackson saw the value of San Francisco Bay in its commercial potential. In 1835, he offered Mexico $5 million in exchange for the bay and the area north of it so that the United States could establish a port of trade and build up whaling businesses.

Given the wealth that the bay could provide, it was perhaps not surprising that Mexico rejected Jackson's offer. In the nineteenth century, whaling was one of the biggest businesses in America; whales were so valued for their oil that they were nicknamed "swimming oil wells." The deep harbors would have also enabled the United States to establish more profitable trade routes across the Pacific Ocean. What's more, there was strong potential for building naval bases in these waters. The topography of the coast on the Texas side was more challenging—the shallow waters made it more difficult for naval operations.

Jackson knew that the California coast would contribute greatly to US prosperity and open a convenient gateway to trade with Asia. While he didn't succeed in acquiring this rich territory in 1835, it would become part of the United States at the end of the Mexican-American War.

In the 1800s, America pushed to gain California from Mexico—its ports were ideal for trade, and in the 1830s, the whaling industry in the West was booming.

taxes as all citizens were. The National Colonization Law of 1824 allowed Mexicans to acquire lands from the missions.

Most of the missions in California remained loyal to the Roman Catholic Church in Spain, so the new Mexican governor proceeded carefully with the goal of secularizing all the missions and reducing the influence of Spain. Under the Secularization Act of 1833, the government of Mexico repossessed most of the territory that the Spanish crown had allotted to missions. Between 1827 and 1835, Mexico attempted to expel all males under the age of sixty who had been born in Spain.

Losing the support of the missions weakened independent Mexico's control of California and the Southwest. Several landowners of Spanish or Mexican heritage, called *californios*, were able to set up successful businesses along the Pacific Coast. Cowhides from the region were highly valued. Many also sold candles and soaps made from animal fat. Californios, however, were dissatisfied with the Mexican government. They paid taxes but felt they received little in return.

The Mexican congress didn't have a clear policy for governing these territories. Organization was poor, and the governing leaders were unqualified, often prioritizing their own self-interest above all else. To buttress the strength of the region, especially with the growing threat of United States encroachment, the Mexican Republic had to increase the population and stabilize local government. It extended the same policy that it had implemented in Texas to the West Coast and Southwest, allowing Anglo-Americans to own land if they became Mexican citizens and converted to Catholicism.

By 1830, 130 Americans had settled in California; that number rose to about 1,300 Americans and 500 Europeans in the next fifteen years. However, just as in Texas, increasing the number of Anglo-Americans in the region would contribute to Mexico's eventual loss of the territory.

The end result of the secularization program was that large plots of former mission land wound up in the hands of local rancheros. Some American Indians received plots of land and livestock as well, but Dr. Gayle Olson-Raymer of Humboldt State University's Department of History writes that the land awarded was too small for them to be able to support themselves. As a result, the rich got richer and the poor got poorer.

CHAPTER FOUR
The United States' First War on Foreign Soil

By 1839, Mexican president Anastasio Bustamante had settled the Pastry War, but his government was unstable and bankrupt. He was deposed in 1841 when Santa Anna returned to power. Tensions grew with Texas over the area between the Nueces and the Rio Grande. Financial troubles continued to plague Mexico as it challenged Texans in the disputed region. Santa Anna tried increasing taxes, but his spending was as extravagant as ever, including staging an over-the-top funeral for the leg he had lost during the Pastry War.

At the same time that Santa Anna resumed leadership in Mexico, John Tyler became president of the United States. He had been serving as vice president when President William Henry Harrison died of pneumonia after just one month in office.

Opposite: With Mexico unwilling to give up territory and the United States pushing to expand under the philosophy of Manifest Destiny, war between the two nations became unavoidable.

One of the biggest issues facing Tyler was the "Texas Question." For Tyler, making the Lone Star Republic a state was a top priority—even though it went against the official position of the Whig Party, of which he was a member. (The Whigs expelled him from the party while he was in office.) He believed that an independent Texas would imperil the Union, while Texas as a state would only strengthen the country—but the nation's division over slavery made annexing Texas problematic. The North did not want to incorporate another pro-slavery state.

Precursors to War

Skirmishes and land disputes continued even after the Texas Revolution had come to an end. These would set the stage for a decisive conflict between the United States and Mexico.

Native Americans Fight for Land Rights

Because Mexico refused to recognize Texan independence after the Treaty of Velasco, many settlers in the newly independent republic were bracing for new attempts at occupation. However, in the latter half of the 1830s, Texans were also facing land disputes with Native Americans, in particular, the Cherokee tribe. The Cherokee had been pushed west by American settlers who took more and more of their ancestral homelands, which included parts of Virginia,

Tennessee, North and South Carolina, Georgia, and Alabama. They started arriving in Texas in the early 1800s, requesting and receiving permission to settle in the region from Spanish authorities.

Between 1838 and 1839, 16,000 to 18,000 Cherokees were forcibly marched, alongside members of other tribes, to a new home in what is now Oklahoma. An estimated 4,000 to 5,000 Cherokee died on what became known as the Trail of Tears. But when Oklahoma became a state in 1907, even this territory would be taken from the Cherokee.

Sam Houston, the first president of the Republic of Texas, had a reputation among the Cherokee for being fair. He promised to give them title to certain lands, and they trusted him. The Texas legislature, however, would not approve these land grants.

Angered by these broken promises, some Cherokee developed allegiances with Mexico, which promised to give them title to their lands. After many tense confrontations, the Cherokee decided to fight for the land, which they considered rightfully theirs. In 1839, several skirmishes between Texans and Native Americans erupted, including the Battle of the Neches on July 16, 1839. The Cherokee had agreed to terms requiring them to leave the area but refused to sign a treaty. As the Cherokee began to leave, however, fighting began and then escalated. About one hundred Native Americans died in the fight; five Texans also died. Texans proceeded to burn the Cherokee's villages and more than 200 acres (80 ha) of cornfields. By the end of 1839, fighting between the Cherokee and the Texans had come to an end.

A Push Toward Annexation

The year 1842 saw several skirmishes as Mexican forces pushed into Texas territory. In the United States, these skirmishes were fueling anger toward Mexico. As the back-and-forth raids continued, President Tyler advocated for annexation. In 1844, his Treaty of Joint Annexation was voted down by the Senate.

Tyler was also working with Mexico to try and purchase California and New Mexico, but Mexico rejected his offers. Still, his persistence on the Texas Question paid off. On March 1, 1845, two days before his last day in office, Tyler had the satisfaction of signing a joint resolution by the House of Representatives and the Senate for annexing Texas. As soon as Tyler signed, the Mexican minister to Washington, Juan Almonte, left the United States, breaking off relations between the two countries. He called the annexation an act of aggression and said that the friendly nation of Mexico was being robbed of its territory.

Tensions Mount as a Waiting Game Starts

Just as the United States was electing a new president— James K. Polk—in 1844, Mexico was again replacing Santa Anna, this time with José Joaquín de Herrera.

Santa Anna was preparing for a war with Texas, but Herrera opposed the timing of this offensive, wanting to first shore up Mexico's weak economy. He called for the recognition of an independent Texas, so long as it did not join the United States. The Mexican congress, however, opposed Herrera on this.

On July 4, 1845, Texas voted to join the United States. Polk moved troops south, to the northeast Nueces River, in order to secure the border; he also sent a navy squadron to the California coast. Zachary Taylor, a sixty-one-year-old general from Kentucky, led four thousand troops to the town of Corpus Christi on the Gulf of Mexico. The soldiers, who represented almost half of the entire US Army, set up their base along the banks of the Nueces, where they began military drills, readying themselves for potential battle. Soldiers, including a fresh-faced twenty-three-year-old named Ulysses S. Grant, were instructed to prepare and wait. They had months to do so—through the fall and into the new year of 1846—before any battle would erupt.

Having gained respect for his fearlessness in battle, Taylor was known as "Old Rough and Ready." He could not stand any of the showy trappings of the military—he favored raggedy pants and a straw hat over a traditional uniform. One soldier said he looked like a farmer off to sell eggs.

Taylor's army, stocked with many young soldiers fresh out of military school, practiced military tactics continuously. One army officer, Samuel Ringgold,

THE POWER OF POLK

Democrat James K. Polk, who became the eleventh president of the United States on March 4, 1845, won by a very slim margin against the Whig Party's Henry Clay, who opposed Texas annexation. Polk declared that incorporating Texas as a slave state would be offset as the country gained territory in the Northwest, which would become an antislavery region. Although Polk served only one term, his decisions helped to define the borders of the continental United States as we know it today.

As the election of 1844 approached, the forty-nine-year-old Polk was not expected to be the Democratic contender for the presidency. Martin van Buren had the early lead, but his rejection of Texas statehood damaged his campaign. Polk, who was the governor of Tennessee, appealed to the South: he was committed to territorial expansion, and he had the support of former president

Andrew Jackson, who was still hugely popular and considered a war hero for his role in the Battle of New Orleans during the War of 1812.

James K. Polk, the eleventh president of the United States, spearheaded the movement for American expansionism and led the country to victory in its war against Mexico.

Polk believed that the United States had rightful claim to the Oregon Territory, which extended far north into what is Canada today. The territory at the time extended up to the latitude line of 54°40′. Polk came up with the popular campaign slogan, "Fifty-four forty or fight!"

Polk made it clear in his inaugural address that the United States planned to expand: "To enlarge its limits is to extend the dominions of peace over additional territories and increasing millions. The world has nothing to fear from military ambition in our Government." Known for a strong work ethic and considered to be a serious-minded man, Polk was determined to make big changes. "I'm the hardest working man in the United States," he would often declare.

By the end of his presidency, Polk had led the country to victory in the Mexican-American War, gaining huge tracts of land to the south, southwest, and west. However, he had also backed down on his "Fifty-four forty or fight!" pledge, negotiating with the British to accept the 49th parallel as the United States' northern dividing line with Canada—a border that remains in place to this day.

Polk toiled so tirelessly, he may have worked himself to death. He died three months after leaving office at the age of fifty-three.

Nicknamed "Old Rough and Ready," General Zachary Taylor did not like the pomp of military. Always willing to fight alongside his men, he led his troops to many victories.

developed an approach called "flying artillery"—a method of battle whereby pieces of artillery could be moved quickly from place to place. He thought this would be a superior way for smaller groups of soldiers to maximize their impact on the enemy. When battle came, he would be proven right.

Deal-Making Collapses

To counter the US buildup, President Herrera sent his armies north to establish camps on the southern side of the Rio Grande. Herrera let it be known that he was open to discussing the Texas dilemma with the United States. In November 1845, Polk sent attorney and businessman John Slidell to negotiate a deal so that the two countries could avoid going to war. Slidell was to present a proposal that the United States would pay off all settlements that Mexico owed US citizens. Mexico owed American citizens more than $3 million for property damage and land seized during several revolutions and uprisings. Pleading bankruptcy, Mexico had stopped payments on these debts.

Slidell demanded that Mexico recognize the Rio Grande as the border between the two nations. The United States also offered up to $30 million for the purchase of California and New Mexico. Polk was keen on annexing California, not just because of his belief in Manifest Destiny, but also because of rumors that Great Britain wanted to control the region.

Before Slidell could get to Mexico to meet face-to-face, Herrera learned of the terms and refused to meet with him. Herrera was said to be open to compromise, but this list of demands seemed to him to be absurd.

After Texas officially became the twenty-eighth US state on December 29, 1845, Herrera lost favor with his people and his authority crumbled. At the beginning of 1846, General Mariano Paredes took over as president. Paredes opposed all compromise with the United States and vowed to lead his country into a "necessary and glorious war."

The Battles Begin

On January 12, 1846, Polk gave the orders for General Taylor to prepare to cross the Nueces River and lead his troops south. On March 8, three thousand troops began their journey in the disputed Tran-Nueces region to a position on the north side of the Rio Grande. (Hundreds of other soldiers stayed behind, stricken with a variety of ailments, from diarrhea to measles; disease was common in the region and felled many a soldier.) At this position on the riverbank opposite the Mexican town of Matamoros, the Americans built a new headquarters of wood and earth, named Fort Texas. For weeks, there was a tense standoff as troops on both sides readied themselves for battle.

By some estimates, the Mexican army was three times larger than American forces. The US government had been forced to recruit soldiers as quickly as possible. Although short of manpower, the army relied on a large number of recent graduates from the United States Military Academy, West Point, and their expertise helped make up for a shortage of men. Mexico, on the other hand, lacked a core of well-trained officers, and many fighters were unprepared peasants who had been conscripted into service. What's more, many of their firearms were old and inefficient.

In Matamoros on April 24, fresh troops led by General Mariano Arista arrived, and 1,600 pushed on across the Rio Grande to establish a position on the northern side, about 28 miles (45 km) upriver from Fort Texas. Now, both Mexican and US forces were in the Trans-Nueces. Two days later, when Taylor sent 80 dragoons (mounted infantry) to Rancho de Carricitos to investigate, a battle commenced. The Mexicans easily overpowered the Americans, killing 11, wounding 7, and capturing 46. Taylor immediately sent a message to the president: "Hostilities may now be considered as commenced."

Meanwhile, Taylor's supplies were on the coast at Point Isabel. He knew it was vital to retrieve them as fast as possible, so he set out with about 2,300 soldiers, leaving 500 behind at Fort Texas. While Taylor and his team made it to Port Isabel without incident, the Mexicans shelled Fort Texas with a steady barrage of cannon fire. After loading 250 wagons with supplies, American troops began the march back to Fort Texas. On the afternoon of May 8, at Palo Alto (near present-day Brownsville, Texas), the Americans came face-to-face with a line of 6,000 Mexican soldiers, outnumbering Taylor and his forces three to one.

Although the odds seemed insurmountable, the Americans gained an advantage. Their superior cannons shot up to four rounds per minute, compared to the

Although vastly outnumbered, American forces led by Zachary Taylor defeated Mexican troops with superior artillery and military tactics at the war's first real battle at Palo Alto in Texas.

slower artillery of the Mexicans, which fired one or two rounds per minute. Meanwhile, Mexican gunpowder was of such poor quality that their cannonballs would often fall short of their mark and roll leisurely by. Finally, the Mexican soldiers were poorly trained in military tactics. These factors combined gave the Americans the upper hand.

Americans advanced on the enemy rapidly using Samuel Ringgold's flying artillery approach to great effect, moving cannons forward fast and then firing. Ringgold, unfortunately, was struck by cannon fire and died three days later. Overwhelmed by the US force, the Mexicans withdrew and regrouped overnight at an old riverbed called Resaca de la Palma that blocked the road to Fort Texas.

Taylor left his wagon train of supplies safely behind, sending his men forward to fight. The Americans had had a chance to rest and eat, but the Mexicans had not eaten for about thirty hours and were demoralized by their loss the previous day. After intense fighting, the Mexicans began to give up, and many retreated toward the Rio Grande and safety on its southern side. A number of them drowned in the river trying to escape. When the smoke had cleared, the United States had lost 45 troops with 97 wounded, while Mexican forces suffered an estimated 158 dead and 228 wounded. These victories set the tone for the war ahead—rattling the confidence of the Mexicans and bolstering the Americans' firm belief that they would win.

Because both Mexico and the United States claimed the Trans-Nueces, each accused the other of spilling blood on their soil and starting the war. Later in December of 1847, Abraham Lincoln, who opposed the war, introduced what became known as the Spot Resolutions in the House of Representatives, questioning whether a spot of blood had really been

Congressman Abraham Lincoln opposed the war with Mexico, and in 1847 he introduced the Spot Resolutions, challenging President Polk to show the spot where blood was spilt on definitively American soil.

shed on soil that definitively belonged to the United States. He accused the United States of provoking war and insisted that Polk only wanted "military glory." The resolutions proved Lincoln's mettle as a politician but won him many pro-war enemies and the temporary nickname of "spotty Lincoln."

War Is Declared

On May 13, 1846, the US Congress voted in favor of Polk's request to declare war on Mexico, authorizing $10 million to fund the war and the recruitment of fifty thousand volunteers.

Mass-circulation newspapers, which covered the victories at Palo Alto and Resaca de la Palma, helped recruitment efforts, and men signed up in droves. Walt Whitman, editor of the *Brooklyn Eagle*, wrote in support of the war as an effort to spread freedom: "What has miserable, inefficient Mexico—with her superstition, her burlesque upon freedom, her actual tyranny by the few over the many—what has she to do with the great mission of peopling the new world with a noble race? Be it ours, to achieve that mission!"

Mexico never declared war against the United States and took the position that it was merely defending its territory. The Mexicans never entered the United States to fight. Without facing any resistance, Taylor and his men crossed the Rio Grande on May 18, 1846, and took the city of Matamoros. With such victories on the US side, many thought the war would be over quickly.

The War on the Western Front

At the same time, in the spring of 1846, tensions between the two countries were building on the western front in California. US Army officer John C. Frémont was leading an expedition in California near Monterey, seeking to drum up patriotic enthusiasm among former US citizens who had settled there. Those with an allegiance to the United States outnumbered the relatively few Mexicans in the region. Frémont warned of an impending war with Mexico and encouraged them to form militias. By May, Frémont received specific orders to set about capturing California for the United States.

On June 14, 1846, two men—Ezekiel Merritt and William Ide—were encouraged by Frémont to lead a takeover of a Mexican outpost in Sonoma and then seize the home of the commander of northern California, Mexican general Mariano Guadalupe Vallejo. They placed him under arrest and forced him to sign an official surrender. Vallejo was actually working secretly with a US representative to help America annex California, but that did not matter to Merritt and Ide. After drinking Vallejo's brandy, they took a piece of linen the size of a large towel, along with some red paint, and created a homemade flag with a crudely drawn bear and red star. They declared that California was now an independent republic, and the images they created remain on the state flag of California today.

For twenty-five days in 1846, Americans took over a Mexican outpost in Sonoma, declaring California independent. Their flag featured a bear and star, which are still on the state flag today.

Frémont then assumed leadership of this growing rebellion, known as the Bear Flag Revolt, and on July 1, he seized the Presidio, a Mexican military fortress in San Francisco.

As hostilities between Mexico and the United States intensified, President Polk sent Commander John Sloat to lead a Pacific squadron of seven battleships into the waters off the coast of California. When Sloat heard about the so-called Bear Flaggers, he took action, seizing the community of Monterey on July 6. The Bear Flaggers replaced their flag with the Stars and Stripes— putting an end to the Republic of California after just three weeks.

The United States now laid claim to all of California north of Santa Barbara. Sloat relinquished his command to Commodore Robert F. Stockton, who sailed south with the navy squadron and readily gained control of San Pedro and Santa Barbara in August of 1846. Mexican forces saw no use in fighting some of these battles. On August 13, Stockton, Frémont, and the California Battalion swept into Los Angeles without a shot being fired. At this time, Stockton finally received official word that the United States was at war with Mexico.

Stockton wrote a note to Polk saying he would serve as interim governor until local elections could be held. He tasked legendary scout and trapper Kit Carson with delivering the note. When Carson crossed paths with Brigadier General Stephen Watts Kearny and his men, who were heading west in the fall, Carson decided to help Kearny with the trek westward. He handed off Stockton's letter to a soldier for delivery to Polk and started the journey back toward the West Coast.

The Invasion of New Mexico

As battles were beginning in Mexico and California, Polk also wanted troops to invade the western territories from the east. So, in May of 1846, as tensions were heating up to the south and along the West Coast, Polk directed Kearny to lead about seventeen hundred troops from Fort Leavenworth in Kansas into New Mexican territory to seize Santa Fe. When Kearny and his men arrived in August after a 900-mile (1,448-km) march, the Mexican forces decided not to put up a fight. Without any shots fired, the United States handily took Santa Fe. Kearny worked to establish a provisional government and reach out to the wary Pueblo Indians, who had resided in the area in relative peace for centuries.

As the United States firmly established itself in the region, however, Native Americans and Mexicans who had been in the area for years hoped they would have some say in the new government, but they did not get it. Resentment against American rule grew. On January 19, 1847, in Taos, a mob of New Mexican and Pueblo Indian rebels kicked in the door where the new governor of New Mexico, Charles Bent, was staying. They murdered Bent and his guards. After scalping Bent, they dragged his body through the town and set fire to stores and homes. Although seven hundred rebels were now controlling Taos, they were no match for a US Army force that arrived soon after and bombarded them with heavy artillery. The creek running through the pueblo turned red with blood. In the end, the army quelled the rebellion, hanging the remaining ringleaders.

Brigadier General Stephen Watts Kearny and his men easily took over Santa Fe, New Mexico, and then with the guidance of legendary scout Kit Carson, continued westward to California.

Forces Push into California

After establishing a base in Santa Fe, Kearny's next mission was to continue another 2,000 miles (3,218 km) to San Diego, where he would meet US naval warships and claim California for the United States. Kearny and about three hundred men set out on September 25, 1846. Among his team was the surveyor William Emory, who was already working to determine possible railway routes that would help bring US settlers to the West. Emory wrote that they encountered Apache Indians along the way who saw them as allies who could rid them of those of Spanish descent. The Apaches told him that the Spanish had been their enemies for hundreds of years. They did not foresee that the Americans would one day take their lands and become their enemies as well.

When Kearny met up with Kit Carson in the journey west, he learned that Stockton and American forces had taken most of California. Based on this information, Kearny sent all but one hundred of his men back to Santa Fe. Kearny, his remaining troops, and their mules were exhausted from their long journey as they approached San Diego. About 30 miles (48 km) from their destination, on December 6, 1846, they confronted Captain Andrés Pico, a Mexican military leader, and a band of about one hundred californios—mounted Mexican troops armed with long, spear-like lances. In the Battle of San Pasquale—one of the last of the Mexican-American War—Kearny and his men valiantly defended themselves but in the end suffered twenty-one dead and fifteen wounded.

Kearny sent two men through the lines get help from Stockton. On January 10, 1847, the US Army secured Los Angeles. Three days later, the Treaty of Cahuenga was signed between Frémont and Pico. As the new year of 1847 began, the territories of California and New Mexico were controlled by the United States, but Mexico still would not surrender, so the battle continued south of the border.

Meanwhile, Back in Mexico

During the summer of 1846, Taylor and his men followed the Rio Grande upstream, taking Reynosa and Camargo. At Camargo, it was clear that the Mexicans were not the only deadly enemy. About fifteen hundred soldiers died there from contaminated water—a number almost equal to the total battle deaths of US soldiers during the Mexican-American War. Actual

THE FIGHTING IRISH IN MEXICO

The largely Irish American San Patricios (or the Saint Patrick's Battalion) joined forces with the Mexicans at Monterrey in their first battle. Numbering about 175, these Irishmen joined Mexico for various reasons, including its allegiance to the Catholic Church and antislavery stance. Mexico also promised higher wages and land grants for fighting. In the United States' final attack on Mexico City, thirty San Patricios were captured and hanged as traitors.

combat deaths in this war were relatively low, but more than ten thousand would die of diseases such as yellow fever.

In September, Taylor decided to press on and take the well-protected walled city of Monterrey, Mexico. Desperate for a victory, Mexico built up a force as large as ten thousand strong, according to some estimates. From September 21 to 23, the Americans rained down heavy artillery on the city, but the Mexicans fought back with ferocity. Both sides were pushed to the limit. After three days of trying to take the city without success, Taylor and his men appeared to be on the brink of retreat. However, at this very point, the Mexicans called for a cease-fire. Mexican forces were allowed to retreat with full honors and keep their firearms (except for a cannon), and Taylor's men took Monterrey. For Mexican soldiers who thought they were so close to a victory, it was a demoralizing loss.

Taylor agreed to a rest in fighting for September and October, angering Polk, who wanted the war to come to a fast end. He believed if Taylor had captured the retreating army, the war would have ended right then and there.

The Return of Santa Anna

Around this time, a familiar Mexican legend had returned to the scene. General Antonio López de Santa Anna had been living in exile in Cuba, but he convinced Polk that if he were brought back to Mexico,

TWO TRANSFORMED NATIONS

When Mexico declared its independence from Spain in 1821, it inherited huge tracts of land in what would become California, New Mexico, Arizona, and Texas, as well as parts of Wyoming, Colorado, and Kansas. When the Treaty of Guadalupe Hidalgo was signed in 1848, bringing an end to the Mexican-American War, the United States acquired more than

This 1826 map shows how vast Mexico (*shown in yellow*) was at the time, including areas that became California, New Mexico, Arizona, and Texas, as well as parts of Wyoming, Colorado, and Kansas.

500,000 square miles (1,294,994 sq km). The border with Texas was established along the Rio Grande rather than the Nueces River, which lay farther to the north. The remaining border ran west across the Colorado River to the Pacific.

With the Gadsden Purchase of 1854, the United States gained an additional 30,000 square mile (77,700 sq km) region of present-day southern Arizona and southwestern New Mexico. The land was necessary for completing a southern transcontinental railroad. The 2,000 mile (3,219 km) border, established in the mid-1800s, extends from the Pacific to the Gulf of Mexico and has remained almost the same since. Today, there is also a maritime border that extends 8 miles (13 km) into the Pacific Ocean and 12 miles (19 km) into the Gulf of Mexico.

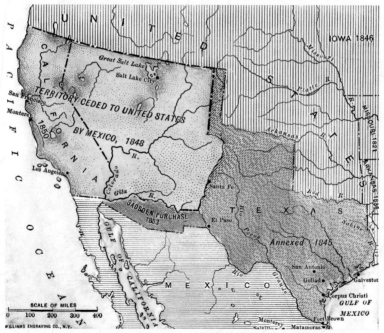

By 1854, the United States had added about a half million square miles to its map, territory acquired from the Mexican-American War, plus 30,000 square miles from the Gadsden Purchase.

he could help end the war on terms that would be agreeable to the United States. Polk arranged for a ship to bring him back to Mexican shores. Santa Anna, however, was ready to betray Polk and fight for his beloved Mexico. Many Mexicans still distrusted Santa Anna, but he seemed to be the only individual who could unite the country, rally the people, and stop the US invasion. In December of 1846, Santa Anna once again became the leader of Mexico.

As Taylor made greater inroads into Mexico alongside other US battalions, Santa Anna looked for the right circumstances to launch a successful attack. Polk, meanwhile, believed that the only way to bring a swift conclusion to the war would be to make a decisive strike against the capital, Mexico City. For this mission, Polk turned to General Winfield Scott. Scott was almost Taylor's opposite when it came to military "show"—he loved uniforms and ceremony and became known as "Old Fuss and Feathers."

At the beginning of the year, Scott took about half of Taylor's men as plans got underway to attack Mexico City. Learning that Taylor was down to about 6,000 troops, mostly inexperienced volunteers, Santa Anna assembled a force of 20,000 to overtake him in January 1847.

Although his troops were not well-trained, Santa Anna felt he needed a victory, and Taylor seemed to be in a vulnerable position. Santa Anna exhausted his soldiers, marching them through the cold, wind, and snow. Their numbers dwindled to 15,000. Taylor got word of the approaching Mexicans and prepared to meet them at Buena Vista. Taylor's men were outnumbered three to one.

Before battle commenced on February 22, Santa Anna gave Taylor a chance to surrender. Fierce fighting commenced, and although Taylor had difficulty holding off the Mexican forces, superior American artillery drove the Mexicans to retreat on the evening of February 23. Santa Anna's men were exhausted—they had not eaten for two days. Estimates vary, but one report put Mexican casualties at 1,500 compared to 700 on the American side—the highest number for a battle so far. It was Taylor's last battle of the campaign—a defeat for Santa Anna and a victory that would secure Taylor's place in history as an American war hero.

CHAPTER FIVE

The Final Fight, and New Borders Drawn

While Santa Anna was off fighting in Buena Vista, a rebellion against the Mexican government broke out in protest over legislation that allowed the government to take money and property from the Catholic Church to fund the war effort. Five national guard regiments joined the Polkos Revolt—a name reportedly derived from the polka, a dance popular among the elite. However, some say they gained the nickname because they were secretly aiding the cause of President Polk. In any case, the revolt would spell the beginning of the end of the Mexican-American War.

The Final Battles

As March came, so did the American soldiers to Veracruz. Winfield Scott arrived with 10,000 men

Opposite: The Mexican-American War came to an end in September 1847 when US general Winfield Scott led troops into Mexico City.

aboard ships for what would be the first amphibious (forces landed from the sea) military attack in US history. The Mexican troops in Veracruz needed backup, but with the Polkos Revolt in Mexico City, no additional help was coming. On March 9, 1847, 10,000 US soldiers landed on the shores of Veracruz without one life being lost. Americans bombarded the city with cannon fire. Forty-year-old army engineer Robert E. Lee, who would go on to lead Confederate military forces in the American Civil War, helped with the placement of the guns and the heavy shelling. After unrelenting bombing, Veracruz surrendered on March 29, 1847.

Santa Anna still would not surrender. He was able to bring forces together again in Mexico City, convincing the church to give a loan that Mexico would repay when the war was over. Putting an end to all revolts, he called on his citizens to unite behind him. In April, Santa Anna set off with 12,000 men toward his hacienda at Encerro, 70 miles (113 km) from Veracruz, where he would establish military headquarters to confront Scott's advancing army. His plan was to drive Scott's army back from an area called Cerro Gordo. If the Americans retreated to the coast, yellow fever would help win the battle. One of Santa Anna's experienced generals recommended placing artillery on a hill called La Atalaya, but Santa Anna would not listen.

When Scott's 8,500 men arrived in mid-April, Lee guided the placement of guns atop La Atalaya, a

Although he was nicknamed "Old Fuss and Feathers," General Winfield Scott was a very successful commander, leading the first amphibious military attack in US history on the port of Veracruz.

position that would prove critical in defeating Santa Anna. By April 19, Scott's army had captured 3,000 of Santa Anna's forces.

Scott wrote to Polk that Mexico no longer had an army, but Santa Anna, having suffered such a devastating defeat, still would not give up. In the United States, citizens celebrated the victory, but many were also growing weary of war, and many continued to speak out against it, including Frederick Douglass and Henry David Thoreau.

In April, Polk sent diplomat Nicholas Trist to travel with Scott's army; his goal was to gain a treaty with Mexico. Trist was able to get a proposal for peace to Santa Anna, but the Mexican congress had made it an act of treason to negotiate with the United States.

The Battle for Mexico City

On August 10, 1847, Winfield Scott marched about 10,000 men into the Valley of Mexico, which surrounds Mexico City, a city of about 300,000 inhabitants. Santa Anna worked feverishly to build up an army of 25,000. Thousands of workers joined the effort. Bells were forged into cannons. Townspeople were asked to dig out their old firearms. Santa Anna marched 7,000 to El Peñón, a large hill near a main road that Santa Anna believed the Americans would need to take for their invasion. However, Scott's method was to always find a way around enemy lines and take the opponent off-guard.

Santa Anna repositioned troops, but again, Scott surprised him. Lee found a passageway through the Pedregal, a 5-mile (8-km) stretch of jagged lava known to tear apart horse hooves. On August 20, the Americans defeated a large battalion of Mexicans, who fled across the Churubusco River to safety behind the fortified walls of Mexico City. The Mexicans inflicted many injuries on the approaching American forces, who suffered more than 1,000 casualties that day, while the Mexicans reportedly lost up to 10,000. The city was now open to American invasion at the gates of Churubusco. Santa Anna sent an emissary to Scott to declare a truce, and the fighting stopped. On August 27, Trist began negotiations with Mexican commissioners, but Santa Anna could not agree to give up territory.

On September 8, fighting resumed, but after less than a week of bloody fighting, Mexican leaders and Santa Anna all agreed to surrender. US troops entered the capital on September 14, 1847.

One out of five soldiers who started with General Scott had died. In the end, more than 5,800 Americans were killed or wounded in battle, and 11,000 soldiers died from diseases. Mexican casualties were greater, with an estimated 25,000 dead troops and civilians. And for every dead soldier, there were often widows and orphans left behind.

The war was not only costly in terms of lives lost— it cost the United States about $75 million.

Although Antonio López de Santa Anna assembled tens of thousands of men for a last stand at the capital of Mexico City, they were no match for the superior firepower of the American forces.

The Boy Heroes (Los Niños Héroes)

On September 13, the day before American forces took over Mexico City, six young Mexican military cadets, ranging in age from thirteen to nineteen, defended Chapultepec Castle, positioned on a hill that protected the capital. When it was apparent that American troops would defeat them, their general ordered them to leave. They refused to give up their posts and vowed to fight to the death. Each young man died in battle that day, including one boy, Juan Escutia, who wrapped himself in the Mexican flag and jumped from the castle rather than have the enemies capture the flag. Today, the Monumento a los Niños Héroes honors these cadets, who died so valiantly. For Mexicans, the boys stand for the patriotism, honor, and courage that make their country a great nation.

THE COLT SIX-SHOOTER

Samuel Colt patented his famous six-cylinder pistol in 1835, but at first, it wasn't in much demand, and he stopped manufacturing the gun in 1842. By 1845, however, the Texas Rangers had discovered his gun and selected it as their weapon of choice. In 1846, the US military placed an order for a thousand units, and Colt was back in business. The Colt six-shooter helped win the war and establish Samuel Colt's reputation as a superior gun manufacturer.

Samuel Colt's invention, the six-shooter pistol, helped win the war. His revolver mechanism enabled a gun to be fired multiple times without reloading. Colt is pictured here holding the pistol.

The War's End

The United States imposed martial law in Mexico City. Major General John Quitman was appointed as the governor of the metropolis. This was the first time that Americans had occupied a foreign capital. The United States demanded that Mexico pay a $3 million tax to maintain its troops in the city. Santa Anna, meanwhile, resigned the presidency and fled to exile in Jamaica. José Manuel de la Peña y Peña, head of Mexico's supreme court, became president of Mexico.

In mid-November, as Trist prepared to negotiate the peace treaty, he received notice from Secretary of State James Buchanan that he had been fired. Polk wanted Mexico to sue for peace. Scott, Peña y Peña, and others urged Trist to stay on. Trist defied the president's orders and started peace negotiations at the beginning of 1848.

On February 2, Trist and Mexican commissioners signed the Treaty of Guadalupe Hidalgo, in which it was agreed that the United States would evacuate all forces from Mexico within three months, would prevent raids by Native Americans, and would pay Mexico $15 million and pay off damage claims against the country. In return, Mexico formally recognized the annexation of Texas. The United States received all territory north of the Rio Grande and across the Colorado River, all the way to the Pacific. California, New Mexico, Nevada, Utah, Texas, and most of

On February 2, 1848, the Treaty of Guadalupe Hidalgo was signed, officially ending the Mexican-American War and acquiring vast territories for the United States.

Arizona were now all territories belonging to the United States.

Polk was furious that Trist had gone against his orders, but he agreed to the terms of the treaty. Polk fired Trist again and docked him any wages owed from October 1847 onward.

The Aftermath

In the end, the deal was enormously empowering for the United States but devastating for Mexico, which lost huge swaths of resource-rich territory. Mexico also had to rebuild cities that were attacked, repair roads, and reestablish businesses, farms, and trade.

While many in the United States celebrated their fulfillment of Manifest Destiny and the growth of the country, others questioned the legitimacy of the war, including Ulysses S. Grant. He wrote in his memoirs, "For myself, I was bitterly opposed to the annexation of Texas, and to this day regard the war, which resulted, as one of the most unjust ever waged by a stronger against a weaker nation. It was an instance of a republic following the bad example of European monarchies, in not considering justice in their desire to acquire additional territory."

Some senators didn't agree with taking so much land from Mexico; others thought that the United States should claim all of Mexico as its territory. Some opposed allowing Mexicans to become citizens. However, with a sense that the country wanted the war to be over, the treaty gained approval in the US Senate in March.

Mexico had to ratify the treaty as well, and—as in the United States—the Mexican congress was divided. Some wanted to return to war rather than give up so much land. Others saw the treaty as a way to regain much of the territory that US forces had already taken in their drive south of the Rio Grande. On May 30, Mexico's congress approved the treaty, bringing the war to an official end.

Polk thought that winning the Mexican-American War and gaining so much territory would help the Democrat candidate Lewis Cass win in the presidential election of 1848. Instead, the Whig candidate—war hero Zachary Taylor—won. Three months after leaving the White House, Polk died.

The Changing Landscape

Mexico went through a period of continued instability after the war. In 1853, Santa Anna returned yet again to claim the presidency. He arranged the Gadsden Purchase, a treaty that gave the United States an additional 30,000 square miles (77,700 sq km) of territory south of the Gila River. Americans wanted the land for completing a transcontinental railroad from California to New Orleans by way of Yuma, Tucson, El Paso, and San Antonio. In return, Mexico received $10 million and an additional $5 million for damages from Native American raids. Giving away more Mexican territory angered many Mexicans, and once again, Santa Anna was deposed.

When liberals came to power in Mexico in 1855, Benito Juárez advocated for national social reforms that would weaken the power of the Catholic Church. He led the way during a period called La Reforma, helping to draft a new constitution and laying the foundations of democracy. He was elected president in 1861.

In part because Mexico lost vast amounts of territory, the country did not grow into a world power comparable to the United States. Still, Mexico would go on to discover that it had large deposits of silver, copper, gold, and other valuable minerals. The country also had vast amounts of timber and petroleum, which in time would become a very valuable commodity.

A Shifting Border

In the two decades following the signing of the Treaty of Guadalupe Hidalgo, the border began to shift of its own accord. Naturally occurring flooding and erosion gradually moved parts of the Rio Grande south. In 1864, a massive flood created a major shift, causing about 600 acres (242 ha) at El Paso to become US territory. The disputed land became known as El Chamizal. After a century of wrangling, President John F. Kennedy agreed to a compromise in 1963, awarding Mexico 366 acres (148 ha) of Chamizal and 71 acres (29 ha) of adjacent Cordova Island. The two nations agreed to share equally in the cost of rechanneling the river, reestablishing the pre-1864 border.

The border, which mostly follows the division established in the Treaty of Guadalupe Hidalgo, remains a defining line between Mexico and the United States. It cuts across many terrains, from urban centers to unpopulated deserts. President Donald Trump has proposed building a border wall for tighter immigration control. Whether the wall is built or not, the border between the two countries will remain a source of debate and concern for generations to come.

The Mexican-American War taught many lessons. Americans united over efforts to both fight and end the war, while Mexicans often fought among themselves as they dealt with an unstable government. The United States invested time into training leaders who pursued successful military tactics and produced weaponry that was superior for the age. With the end of the war, Mexico could focus on becoming a stronger, more democratic nation.

In the end, the boundary established by the Mexican-American War (and the Gadsden Purchase, soon to follow) is nearly the same as that which divides the two nations today. The border serves as a checkpoint between the countries and now features a variety of fencing, more than thirty border patrol stations, and twenty-five legal ports of entry. Although the unemployment rate in Mexico has been lower—at between 3 and 4 percent—than in the United States in

The peace treaty that ended the Mexican-American War gave Mexicans the option of remaining in the annexed regions as US citizens or moving back to Mexico. About eighty thousand decided to stay.

For those Mexicans who did become citizens, life was not always easy. While they retained the right to their language, religion, and culture, many faced prejudice because of differences in their culture and physical appearance from Anglo-Americans. They were often discriminated against, given jobs with low wages,

Millions of people of Mexican heritage—such as these students in south Texas—live in the United States today, making vital contributions to the culture of the United States.

and harassed. In 2015, the *New York Times* reported that between 1848 and 1928, thousands of Mexicans were lynched or murdered by mobs. These attacks were widespread, occurring throughout Arizona, California, New Mexico, and Texas, as well as in states farther from the border, such as Wyoming and Nebraska.

To keep the land that they had lived on for years in what was now the United States, Mexicans had to file paperwork proving ownership. Sometimes there was no written documentation, and people lost homes and property that had been theirs for generations.

Over time, Mexican Americans have become part of the vital fabric of the country. They have filled countless jobs and served the country honorably in World War II, Korea, Vietnam, and other conflicts. Despite all this, according to a feature on PBS, Mexican Americans are still often treated like second-class citizens, and because of these challenges, they still lag behind other ethnic groups when it comes to education, income, and homeownership. Even so, Mexicans and Mexican Americans continue to pursue the American dream. With more than eighteen million Mexican Americans living in the United States today, they are the fastest-growing minority group in the country.

recent years, the jobs being created are often very low paying. That's why millions of Mexicans have crossed into the United States without documentation, seeking better opportunities. That trend might be changing, however, as a poll from the Pew Research Center in 2015 showed that more Mexican immigrants were returning to Mexico than were entering the United States as economic conditions grew stronger there.

While there are tensions between the two countries regarding illegal immigration, billions of dollars in commerce travel between the United States and Mexico. For example, Mexico is by far the leading supplier of fresh vegetables to the United States; nearly 11.6 billion pounds (5.26 billion kilograms) of vegetables valued at $5.6 billion were imported from Mexico in 2016, according to the US Department of Agriculture Economic Research Service.

In addition to determining a border, the Mexican-American War gave the United States 320 million acres (129.5 million ha) of land, an acquisition that would help make the country an international superpower with territory stretching from the Pacific to the Atlantic. Today, the border established by the war is internationally recognized and likely to stay in place for generations to come.

- **1803** In a transaction called the Louisiana Purchase, the United States acquires about 827,000 square miles (2,141,920 sq km) of land west of the Mississippi River from France for $15 million.

- **1816** James Monroe is elected president, ushering in the Era of Good Feelings, a time of unity and hope for the United States.

- **1817** Andrew Jackson leads an incursion into Florida, beginning the First Seminole War.

- **1819** In the Adams-Onís Treaty, Spain cedes Florida to the United States and defines boundaries with Spain's western territories. Spain gives up claims in the Northwest.

- **1821** Mexico becomes independent from Spanish rule.

- **1823** President James Monroe announces the Monroe Doctrine, a US policy opposing any further European colonization in the Western Hemisphere.

- **1824** On October 4, the United Mexican States, or Estados Unidos Mexicanos, becomes a representative federal republic. John Quincy Adams is elected US president.

- **1825** Stephen Austin successfully settles three hundred families in Texas.

- **1828** Andrew Jackson is elected president of the United States.

- **1829** Mexican president Vicente Guerrero Saldaña, the first man of African heritage to be elected president of a North American country, emancipates all slaves in Mexico. Many communities in Texas seek and receive an exemption.

- **1835** The first shots of the Texas Revolution are fired in Gonzales.

- **1836** After the legendary battle at the Alamo and the Goliad Massacre, Texas declares itself the independent Lone Star Republic. Mexico refuses to recognize Texas's independence.

- **1838** France goes to war with Mexico over unpaid debts in what will be known as the Pastry War.

- **1840** William Henry Harrison is elected US president.

- **1841** Antonio López de Santa Anna returns to Mexican presidency. John Tyler becomes US president when Harrison dies after just one month in office.

- **1844** James K. Polk is elected US president.

- **1845** The US government offers Texas statehood in March; in retaliation, Mexico breaks off diplomatic relations with America. In July, Texas votes to become the twenty-ninth state, and

Polk moves troops under the leadership of Zachary Taylor into southern Texas.

- **1846** The Mexican-American War begins. US troops win significant victories in Palo Alto and Resaca de la Palma and claim the territories of California and New Mexico. In December, Santa Anna once again rises to power in Mexico to lead the final war efforts.

- **1847** In February, Santa Anna leads fifteen thousand men to fight Zachary Taylor's troops in the Battle of Buena Vista, outnumbering them three to one. Santa Anna is defeated but both sides suffer high casualties. In March, General Winfield Scott makes the first amphibious military invasion in Veracruz. In September, Scott and his men take Mexico City.

- **1848** Mexico and the United States sign the Treaty of Guadalupe Hidalgo in February. In November, General Zachary Taylor is elected president.

- **1854** In the Gadsden Purchase, the United States acquires an additional 30,000 square miles (77,700 sq km) of Mexican land south of Arizona and New Mexico.

allegiance Loyalty.

Anglo-American A North American whose native language is English and whose ethnic or cultural background is European.

annexation The incorporation of a new territory into a city, state, or country.

artillery Large-caliber weapons used in warfare.

authoritarian Characterized by a concentration of power in a ruler or a small group of elites who deny freedoms and demand that people obey their wishes.

barrage A heavy bombardment of artillery fire.

burlesque In this case, a mockery; a work that makes fun of something.

conscript To force someone by law to enlist in the armed forces.

convert To change one's religious faith.

depose To forcibly remove someone from office.

dragoon A soldier who rides on a horse; a cavalryman.

empresario Spanish for "entrepreneur" or "businessperson," it refers to—in this case—someone who has been granted the right to settle on land in exchange for recruiting and overseeing new settlers.

hacienda A large estate or plantation in a Spanish-speaking country.

interim Temporary or stopgap.

obstinacy Stubbornness.

perfidious Deceitful.

presidio A fortified military settlement.

prosthetic An artificial body part.

ranchero Someone who farms, works, and/or owns a ranch, especially in Mexico or the southwestern United States.

retaliatory Something done in response to an action with the purpose of getting revenge.

secularize To transfer from religious influence or connection to civil use, unassociated with any religion.

treachery Betrayal of trust.

usurp To illegally or forcefully take over a position of power.

viceroy A ruler in a colony acting on the authority of a sovereign, king, or queen.

Books

Cantor, Carrie Nichols. *The Mexican War: How the United States Gained Its Western Land*. Chanhassen, MN: The Child's World, 2003.

Eisenhower, John S. D. *So Far from God: The U.S. War with Mexico*. Norman, OK: University of Oklahoma Press, 2000.

Mills, Bronwyn. *America at War: U.S.-Mexican War*. New York: Chelsea House, 2010.

Sonneborn, Liz. *The Mexican-American War: A Primary Source History of the Expansion of the Western Land of the United States*. New York: Rosen Publishing, 2005.

Tenzer, Ruth Feldman. *The Mexican-American War*. Minneapolis: Lerner Publications, 2004.

Websites

A Guide to the Mexican War

loc.gov/rr/program/bib/mexicanwar/

This Library of Congress digital collection compiled by Kenneth Drexler contains a wide variety of material associated with the Mexican-American War, including manuscripts, maps, broadsides, pictures, sheet music, books, and government documents.

Mexican-American War

history.com/topics/mexican-american-war

The History Channel offers comprehensive coverage of all the major episodes of the Mexican-American War, including video clips.

The Texas State Historical Association

https://tshaonline.org/handbook/online

This nonprofit organization keeps a very detailed account of Texas history, including information on the Texas Revolution, statehood, and the war with Mexico.

Videos

The Alamo

www.imdb.com/title/tt0318974

Directed by John Lee Hancock and produced by Touchstone Pictures in 2004, this account of the attack on the Alamo stars Billy Bob Thornton and Dennis Quaid.

The Mexican-American War

vimeo.com/64537022

Hosted by Oscar de la Hoya and produced by History Channel and A&E Home Video in 2008, this two-hour documentary on the war features reenactments and interviews with both Mexican and American historians.

One Man's Hero

imdb.com/title/tt0102595

Directed by Lance Hool and produced by Arco Films in 1999, this movie is a fictional account of the St. Patrick's Battalion.

U.S.-Mexican War

pbs.org/kera/usmexicanwar/index_flash.html

This PBS documentary from 2006 shows how the war transformed a continent and forged a new identity for its people.

BIBLIOGRAPHY

Alcaraz, Ramon. "A Controversial War." Digital History, 1850. http://www.digitalhistory.uh.edu/disp_textbook. cfm?smtID=3&psid=553.

Bates, Christopher G. *The Early Republic and Antebellum America: An Encyclopedia of Social, Political, Cultural, and Economic History.* New York: Routledge, 2010.

Cantor, Carrie Nichols. *The Mexican War: How the United States Gained Its Western Land.* Chanhassen, MN: The Child's World, 2003.

Carlson, Johnni. "How Important Is the Rio Grande for Mexico and the United States?" LifePersona, July 24, 2017. https://www.lifepersona.com/how-important-is-the-rio-grande-for-mexico-and-the-united-states.

Columbia Encyclopedia. "Rio Grande." Encyclopedia.com. Accessed January 17, 2018. http://www.encyclopedia.com/places/united-states-and-canada/us-physical-geography/rio-grande-us-river.

Colorado's Water Plan. "Rio Grande River Basin." Accessed January 17, 2018. https://www.colorado.gov/pacific/cowaterplan/rio-grande-river-basin.

Eisenhower, John S. D. *So Far from God: The U.S. War with Mexico.* Norman, OK: University of Oklahoma Press, 2000.

Encyclopædia Britannica. "Battle of Buena Vista." Accessed January 17, 2018. https://www.britannica.com/event/Battle-of-Buena-Vista.

Encyclopedia.com. "Empresario System." 2003. http://www.encyclopedia.com/history/dictionaries-thesauruses-pictures-and-press-releases/empresario-system.

Flank, Lenny. "The Pastry War: How a French Bakery Caused a War in Mexico." *Daily Kos*, July 10, 2014. https://www.dailykos.com/stories/2014/7/10/1301627/-The-Pastry-War-How-a-French-Bakery-Caused-a-War-in-Mexico.

Leanos, Reynaldo. "This Underground Railroad Took Slaves to Freedom in Mexico." PRI's *The World*, March 29, 2017. https://www.pri.org/stories/2017-03-29/underground-railroad-took-slaves-freedom-mexico.

Miller, Robert Ryal. "The Aftermath of War: The War Between the United States and Mexico." California State University, Hayward/PBS.org. Accessed January 17, 2018. http://www.pbs.org/kera/usmexicanwar/aftermath/war.html.

Mills, Bronwyn. *America at War: U.S.-Mexican War*. New York: Chelsea House, 2010.

Minster, Christopher. "Biography of Stephen F. Austin." ThoughtCo, September 22, 2017. https://www.thoughtco.com/biography-of-stephen-f-austin-2136243.

Office of the Historian. "Acquisition of Florida: Treaty of Adams-Onis (1819) and Transcontinental Treaty (1821)." United States Department of State. Accessed January 17, 2018. https://history.state.gov/milestones/1801-1829/florida.

Olson-Raymer, Gayle. "Mexican Occupation and American Conquest." Humboldt State University's History Department. Accessed January 17, 2018. http://users.humboldt.edu/ogayle/hist383/Mex_Americans.html.

Osborn, Carolyn. "The Changing Mexico-US Border." Worlds Revealed: Geography and Maps, Library of Congress, December 18, 2015. https://blogs.loc.gov/maps/2015/12/the-changing-mexico-u-s-border.

Peace, Roger. "The United States-Mexican War, 1846–1848." United States Foreign Policy History and Resource Guide. Accessed January 17, 2018. http://peacehistory-usfp.org/US-Mexican-War.

People's World. "Today in Latino History: Mexico Becomes a Republic." October 4, 2013. http://www.peoplesworld.org/article/today-in-latino-history-mexico-becomes-a-republic.

BIBLIOGRAPHY

Sonneborn, Liz. *The Mexican-American War: A Primary Source History of the Expansion of the Western Land of the United States*. New York: Rosen Publishing, 2005.

Tenzer, Ruth Feldman. *The Mexican-American War*. Minneapolis: Lerner Publications, 2004.

Texas Beyond History, "Battles for the Nueces Strip." June 30, 2003. https://www.texasbeyondhistory.net/forts/clark/battles.html.

Texas State Historical Association. "Constitution Proposed in 1833." Accessed January 17, 2018. https://tshaonline.org/handbook/online/articles/mhc09.

———. "Goliad Massacre." Accessed January 17, 2018. https://tshaonline.org/handbook/online/articles/qeg02.

Tucker, Spencer. *The Encyclopedia of the Mexican-American War*. Goleta, CA: ABC-CLIO, 2012.

VandeCreek, Drew. "Military Campaigns." Northern Illinois University, 2014. http://lincoln.lib.niu.edu/mexicanamerican/military.

West, Elliott. "Spanish Missions (in U.S. History)." Scholastic. Accessed January 17, 2017. https://www.scholastic.com/teachers/articles/teaching-content/spanish-missions-us-history.

Wishart, David. "Adams-Onís Treaty." Encyclopedia of the Great Plains, University of Nebraska-Lincoln, 2011. http://plainshumanities.unl.edu/encyclopedia/doc/egp.ha.002.

INDEX

Page numbers in **boldface** are illustrations

Adams, John Quincy, 12
Adams-Onís Treaty
    (Transcontinental Treaty),
    12–14, 17
agriculture, 40–42, 44
Alamo, the, 25–28
amphibious landing, 6, 82
Austin, Stephen, **19**, 19–20,
    20, 22–25

Bastrop, Baron de, **19**
border, US-Mexican
    early, 14, 17, 30, 42,
        61, **76**, **77**
    shifts in after war, 94–95
    today, 6–7, 9, **9**, **39**,
        77, 95, 98
Buchanan, James, 6, 90
Bustamante,
    Anastasio, 29, 53

California, 24, 57
    becomes a state, 48
    fighting in, 68–70, 73–74
    gold in, 44–45
    as part of New Spain
        and Mexico, 45–48,
        50–51, 56, 61, 76
    Republic of, 68–70, **69**
Carson, Kit, 70, 73
Cherokee tribe, 54–56
Civil War, 6–7, 82
Colt, Samuel, 88, **89**
Comanche tribe, 18–19, 47
Crockett, Davy, 25, **26**, 27

disease, 47, 62, 74–75

empresario system, 18, 22

Florida, 11–12
France, 10, 12, 32–35, 53
Frémont, John C., 68–70, 74

Gadsden Purchase, 77, 93, 95
gold, 36, 44, 94
Goliad Massacre, 28
Grant, Ulysses S., 6–7, 57, 92

Herrera, José Joaquín de,
    56–57, 61–62
Houston, Sam, 25, 27–
    28, 30, 55

Irish American fighters, 74
Iturbide, Agustín de, 16–17

Jackson, Andrew, 12, 25,
    29, 48, 58

Kearny, Stephen Watts,
    70–71, **72**, 73–74

Lee, Robert E., 6–7, 82, 85
Lincoln, Abraham, 7,
    65–67, **66**
Los Niños Héroes, 88
Louisiana Purchase,
    10, **11**, 13

Manifest Destiny, 5, 61, 92
Mexican Americans,
    96, 96–97
Mexican-American War,
    34–35, **52**, **64**

aftermath, 92–95
causes/precursors, 5,
  35, 54–62
end of, 76, 85, 90–93
final battles, 81–89
invasion of New Mexico,
  70–71, 74
opposition to, 7, 65–
  67, 84, 92
start of, 62–67
western front, 68–
  70, 73–74
Mexico
  in debt, 32–35, 53, 61
  independence, 16–17, 32,
    45, 47–51, 76
  loss of land, 7–8, 70,
    76–77, 90–94
  maps, **4**, **76**, **77**
  new settlements, 17–22
Mexico City, 23, 78, **80**, 82,
  84–85, **86–87**, 88, 90
mining, 44–46
missions, 45–51
Missouri Compromise, 14
Monroe, James, 10–11, 18

Native Americans, 12, **13**,
  16, 18–19, 23, 40, **41**,
  42–44, 46–47, 51, 71,
  73, 90, 93
  fight for land rights, 54–56
natural resources, 36–
  51, 92, 94
Nueces River, 14, 29–30,
  36–38, **37**, 41–42, 53,
  57, 62, 77

Palo Alto, 63, **64**, 67

Pastry War, 32–35, 53
Polk, James K., 7, 56–59,
  58, 61–62, 67, 69–71,
  75–78, 81, 84, 90–93
Pueblo Indians, 40, **41**, 71

ranchers/ranching, 18, 36,
  42–44, **43**, 46
Ringgold, Samuel, 57–61, 65
Rio Grande, 19, 21, 29–30,
  32, 36–42, **38**, 53, 61–
  63, 65, 67, 74, 77, 93–94
Roman Catholicism, 12, 16,
  18, 20, 46–47, 50–51,
  74, 81, 94

Santa Anna, Antonio López,
  17, 23–29, 33, 53,
  56–57, 75–79, 81–85,
  90, 93–94
Scott, Winfield, **81**, 81–
  85, **83**, 90
Seminole Indians, 12, **13**
slavery, 7–8, 12, 14, **15**, 21,
  30, 54, 58
Slidell, John, 61
Sloat, John, 69–70
Spain, 11
  Mexican independence,
    16–17, 32, 45,
    47–51, 76
  New Spain, 13–14, 45–46
  sells Florida, 12
Stockton, Robert F.,
  70, 73–74

Taylor, Zachary, 6, 57, **60**,
  62–63, 65, 67, 74–75,
  78–79, 93

Texas
    fight for independence,
        21–29, 35, 54
    independence, 29–30,
        36, 54, 57
    part of New Spain, 14, 47
    Republic of, 30, **31**, 55
    settlements in, 19–22, 51
    statehood, 54, 56–
        58, 61, 90
Texas Revolution, 23–29,
    26, 33, 54
trade between US and
    Mexico, 8, 98
Trans-Nueces, 37, 42,
    62–63, 65

Treaty of Guadalupe Hidalgo,
    76, 90–95, **91**
Trist, Nicholas, 84–85, 90–92
Tyler, John, 53–54, 56

United States
    desire for expansion, 5–6,
        10–12, 58–59, 92
    land gained after war, 5, 7,
        59, 76–77, 90–94, 98
    maps, **4**, **76**, **77**

whaling, 36, 48, **49**

Don Rauf is the author of more than thirty nonfiction books, including *Killer Lipstick and Other Spy Gadgets*, *Schwinn: The Best Present Ever*, *American Inventions*, *The French and Indian War*, *The Rise and Fall of the Ottoman Empire*, *George Washington's Farewell Address*, and *Historical Serial Killers*. He lives in Seattle with his wife, Monique, and son, Leo.